BOOKS BY JOHN HOLLANDER

Poetry

Harp Lake   1988
In Time and Place   1986
Powers of Thirteen   1983
Blue Wine and Other Poems   1979
Spectral Emanations: New and Selected Poems   1978
Reflections on Espionage   1976
Tales Told of the Fathers   1975
The Head of the Bed   1974
Town and Country Matters   1972
The Night Mirror   1971
Types of Shape   1969
Visions from the Ramble   1965
Movie-Going   1962
A Crackling of Thorns   1958

Criticism

Rhyme's Reason   1981
    A Guide to English Verse
The Figure of Echo   1981
    A Mode of Allusion in Milton and After
Vision and Resonance   1975
    Two Senses of Poetic Form
The Untuning of the Sky   1961
    Ideas of Music in English Poetry 1500–1700

For Children

*The Immense Parade on Supererogation Day
    and What Happened to It*   1972
The Quest of the Gole   1966

HARP LAKE

HARP LAKE

POEMS BY

JOHN HOLLANDER

ALFRED A KNOPF
New York 1988

THIS IS A BORZOI BOOK
PUBLISHED BY ALFRED A. KNOPF, INC.

Library of Congress Cataloging-in-Publication Data

Hollander, John.
  Harp lake.

  I. Title.
  PS3515.03485H37   1988   811'.54   88–45266
  ISBN 0–394–57247–5
  ISBN 0–394–72051–2 (pbk.)

Some poems in this work were originally published in the following publications: *America, Denver Quarterly, Grand Street, Iowa Review, Journal of Garden History, The New Republic, The New York Review of Books, The Paris Review, Partisan Review, Raritan, River Styx, South Coast Poetry Journal, Thames Poetry, The Times Literary Supplement, 2 Plus 2,* and *The Yale Review.*

"From the Old City" and "From the Inner City" were originally published in *Cumberland Poetry Review.*

"Baigneuse," "Desires of Here and There," "A Glimpse of Proserpina," "Indian Summer, 1975," "Kitty and Bug," "Looking Ahead," "The Mad Potter," and "New Graveyard in New Jersey" were originally published in *The New Yorker.*

"Co-ordinating Conjunction" and "For a Tall Headstone" were originally published in *Poetry.*

"Montdesir" was originally published as "The Summit" in *The Poetry Miscellany.*

"To a Forest Pool" was originally published in *Shenandoah.*

"To Elizabeth Bishop" was originally published in *Looking Ahead,* published by Nadja, 1982.

"Ontology is a Matter of Midnight" was originally published in *For Robert Penn Warren,* published by Palaemon Press, 1980.

"Kinneret" was originally published in a limited edition by Eighty Seven Press, 1986.

Grateful acknowledgment is made to the following for permission to reprint previously published material:

Taylor & Francis Ltd.: the poem "Ave Aut Vale" by John Hollander, originally published in *Word & Image,* Volume 2, Number 1, page 57. Copyright © 1986 by *Taylor & Francis Ltd.* Reprinted by permission of *Taylor & Francis Ltd.*

University of California Press: the poem "The Widener Burying-Ground" from *The Figure of Echo: A Mode of Allusion in Milton and After* by John Hollander. Copyright © 1981. Reprinted by permission of the *University of California Press.*

Manufactured in the United States of America
First Edition

FOR GEORGE KATEB

CONTENTS

HARP LAKE

Notes on some of the poems will be found on page 93

KINNERET

As the dry, red sun set we sat and watched
  Them bring the fish in from the harp-shaped lake.
At night my life, whose every task is botched,
  Dreams of far distant places, by mistake.

They tunnelled through the mountains to connect
  The raging ocean with the inland sea.
Dreaming of you, I wander through some wrecked
  Historic region of antiquity.

We played unknowing for the highest stakes
  All day, then lost when night was "drawing nigh."
The dark pale of surrounding hemlocks makes
  Stabs at transcendence in the evening sky.

Out on the lake at night one understands
  How the far shore's more distant than a star.
The music playing right into my hands,
  I took the measure of my dark guitar.

Beauty? the dolphins leap. But for the truth,
  The filtering balein of the great whale.
Age? it's more gullible than flashing youth:
  The ending swallows the beginning's tale.

Far from the freeway and its hoarse, sick roaring,
  He can still listen to the wildwood's sigh.
Across the world the shattering rain was pouring:
  Tears merely glistened in my childhood's eye.

Out of the depths I call for you: the water
  Drowns it, as if that sound were its own name.
Enisled in height, she learned what had been taught her:
  From closer up, the sky was more of the same.

Her thought was silent, but the darkness rang
   With the strong questions of a headlight's beam.
He walked around the lake: the water sang
   An undersong as if it were a stream.

The wind was working on the laughing waves,
   Washing a shore that was not wholly land.
I give life to dead letters: from their graves
   Come leaping even X and ampersand.

Below, the dialect of the market-place,
   All dark *o*'s, narrowed *i*'s and widened *e*'s.
Above, through a low gate, this silent space:
   The whitened tomb of wise Maimonides.

Only a *y*, stupidly questioning,
   Separates what is yours from what is ours.
Only mute aspiration now can sing
   Our few brief moments into endless hours.

The merest puddle by the lowest hill
   Answers the flashing sunlight none the less.
I harp on the two flowing themes of still
   Water and jagged disconnectedness.

I lay in a long field; eleven sheep
   Leapt from a barge onto the grass, and fed.
She cleared the wall and leapt into my sleep,
   Riding her piebald mare of night and dread.

Dressed like their foes, nomadic and unkempt,
   The emperor's legion crept across the stream.
Only as her great rival could she attempt
   The soft parapets of her lover's dream.

The voice of the Commander rang in us;
  Our hearts in stony ranks echoed his shout.
The cold, bare hills have no cause to discuss
  What the thunder among them is about.

Musing at sundown, I recall the long
  Voyages across shoreless seas of sand.
Shuddering at dawn, I call out for your song,
  O isle of water in the broad main of land.

What speck of dust fell on my page of strife
  And mixed its coughing with the prose of breath?
The pensive comma, hanging on to life?
  The full stop that sentences us to death.

From his blue tomb the young sun rises and
  The marble whitecaps pass like dancing stones.
A boy, somewhere in an old, arid land,
  Sat carving spoons out of his father's bones.

Windward, the sun; a galley on our lee
  Rolls gently homeward; now its sail is gone.
This miracle the moonlight once gave me:
  The sky lay still; the broad water walked on.

What cannot be seen in us as we stare
  At the same stretch of ordinary bay?
Her constant dreaming of the Immermeer,
  My half-lost moment on the Harfensee.

In bright, chaste sunlight only forms are seen:
  Off-color language gives the world its hue.
Only in English does the grass grow green;
  In ancient Greece the dogs were almost blue.

The bitten-into fig does, without doubt,
  Show forth that blushing part of which we've heard.
Resemblance turns our language inside-out:
  Pudenda is a self-descriptive word.

He fought Sloth in her arbitrary den,
  And grew bored long before he could defeat her.
I stop—something is too pedestrian
  About the iambs in this kind of meter.

Footsore, his argument gave out and slept
  In the unmeasured vale of meditation.
In marked but quiet waves the water kept
  Time with the heartbeats of an old elation.

This night in which all pages are the same
  Black: the Hegelians must shut up shop.
It seemed when, smiling, you called out my name
  The humor of the noon would never stop.

He parsed his schoolboy Greek, the future more
  Vivid, where rich, strange verbs display emotion.
My glass of dark wine drained, from the dim shore
  I scan the surface of a sparse, gray ocean.

They built beside a chilly mountain lake
  The prison of particularity.
The sun is blind now; only the stars awake
  To see the whole world mirrored in the sea.

The sea's a mere mirror wherein you see
  Something of the gray face of the high sky.
Far from shore, the dark lake relays to me
  The lie of the old, silent land nearby.

The everlastingness of childhood's summer
  Evenings itself skyrockets and is gone.
As if great age would evermore become her
  The far-lit winter night reigns on and on.

Snows on the far, long mountain in the north,
  Seen from the lake, are never reflected there.
Gazing at distance, I keep setting forth
  Unwittingly into the thoughtless air.

We stand our ungiving ground, our unpaid mission
  To creep through fields or scamper across the town.
Still at last, supine, we learn what position
  Earth took on the great issues of up and down.

A kingfisher flashed by them on their lee
  To lead their thoughts toward a blue yet once more.
My tears blur world and water and I see
  Each seed of flickering lake, each drop of shore.

The dry, unsinging river that runs south:
  Somewhere along it we must some day cross.
The memory of music in my mouth
  Sticks to my silence now like leaves, like moss.

Some husbandman will plow where now I row;
  My lively wake will be the long dead road.
Drowning our songs, the river will flood and go
  Mad, as if flowing were itself a goad.

My mind's eye, wearied of distrust, soon turned
  To surfaces, of which it then grew fond.
She meditated on the mud that churned
  Up from the fruitful bottom of the pond.

Down in undreaming deeps the heavy carp
  Fed, while above the shining surface trembled.
Was it my voice that spoke for the bright harp?
  Or was it a heart the singing lake resembled?

Some say I mutter; some, that I reconditely
  Shout: but meanings, like words, like air, expand.
Some fragments hurt you when you grasp them tightly,
  Some feel as if they were part of your hand.

Every dog has his day, and the worm turns
  Nasty within the hard, absorbing grave.
The heat of August threatens as it burns
  Our hearts with the dead cold of winter's cave.

The wind turned to the hard hills and wondered
  At their cold heads and then began to hum.
My white and faulty mortar should not have sundered
  Under the grinding of this cardamom.

Pale cliffs descend below the sea and steep
  In the full silence, calm and unconfounded.
He broke through the thrumming surface of his sleep
  As if some lake-shaped instrument had sounded.

FROM THE OLD CITY

Stones hewn from sunset, from low
Hills echoed by low-built domes,
Holding wise, old eyes below
Wall-level: so hills, domes, bare
Temples of lowered heads, keep
Their moderate height. And so
Full, tall cupolas raise up
Even their shoulders in pride
Of possession, biting out
Their chunks of sky in triumph
Among high, thin minarets
And campaniles. But the space
Inside is full of sighing.
The hollow Sepulchre, and
That allusive Rock from which
The Prophet was plucked skyward
And father Isaac was not,
Stand braced on a truss of swords
Rusted bright. Mortared with
Dropped zealousness and muddied
Blood, both crowned with high domes set
On cylinders and banded
With squinting eyes turned every
Which way—these have claimed the day.
These hold the tent, the robe or
Whatever it is of blue
Overhead. These fly the flag
Of whatever the weather.

Low-domed, though, the old houses
Peer above their walls, knowing
What they know, their wailing long
Ceased, old tears dried up to this
Wisdom: *There was only one
Temple once; it was given*

Only one revision, one
Second chance, and then it passed
On, beyond its finest shards
Into the continuing
Place within, the center of
The true City of Plurals.
Knowing this, all these flattened
Curves disdain the sunlit domes,
Their immensities of gold
And blood, their derivative
Fables of the emptiness
Of holy places. False domes.
Sometimes in the jostle of
Low, overarched market streets
At noon, a high romance of
Resolution momently
Emerges: as that a Djinn
Of some great kind would descend,
Wide-winged and hilarious,
And seizing the false godhead
By the temples, in between
Thumb and forefinger, would fling
It all to Gehenna, down
Among mud and broken stones,
A few goats and small schoolboys
Playing soccer on a patch
Of clear, squared-off bottom ground.

But like the last wraparound
Of a length of closing scroll,
Flying engines of funny
Angelic outrage are too
Easy to imagine. It
Is when midnight washes blood
Out of her stones, reclaiming
A dark commonality
Of rock and sky, that the old
City disrobes and shows off

Her youth—gently curving breasts
Of a slim body, laid low
Along a small hill—that the false
Corpus of age falls away
Before the truth that was and
Is now and ever shall be
Figured, not builded of stone.

This the sojourners know. This
The wanderer, wondering,
Keeps under his hat, heeding
Warnings of the sun, the wind,
And the water, but who comes
Upon the rock and the sky
Afresh, and the past of sand
And truth lying in spaces
Too small for anything but
Trope, lying in and among
The illimitable grains,
Idols themselves of golden
Specks gathered across worlds of
Darkness, from deserted stars.

FROM THE INNER CITY

All this is recent rubble,
Too young to have been ruined
So soon, before the laughing
Series of sunlit ages
Fills the vacancy of lots
Of destruction with meaning.
Then broken building-shells will
Be overgrown with the green
Of history; then lessons
About burning will have long
Been learnt, and long forgotten.

Behold the metropolis
Within, unhappier far
Beyond dilapidation:
Not the heart of the city
But its blasted fistula,
Hard by the river of cars
That bubbles past, across which
Darkening Time stands in wait
For a last fire which will do
His work for him, polishing
Off the few bricks left to stand.
It is as if some war saw
Its six days' work, that it was
Good, and then abandoned it
All to the jackals of peace.

But beyond the cars and roads
Of water, resting in a
State of grass I have recalled
Thee: my opened book now hung
From one of these trees, its leaves
Silent on the windless bough,
I remember now the old

City that is the inward
Place of wisdom. If its walls
Never rose to the music
Of enterprise, they never
Fell to any kind of fire.

They protect and imprison
My heart, that the place of thought
May yet flourish in their midst.
There, where stone brings forth figures
And words arise from chimneys
In the airy mornings, light
Itself watches—not without
Amazement—what it has wrought.

THE FOUR AGES

I

Terribly unimportant kings
Grimly gave each other rings.

II

That was when the rings had become truly golden
By being remembered dimly and made bright in
The Great Fable that was itself the age, the age
That was not the poor first but the rich harvesting
Of cold grain smitten in the wind by early stones.
The light of dawn was all eaten up in hunger
For beginning again, when the vivid eye lived
At subsistence level; it was only later
On in the day when we saw what shining was all
About, and when we could afford comparisons
Of this with that and then and now, and time
And space lay all about us waiting to be used.
We remember the first age now only to give
The lie, which is its great truth, to this later one.

III

After that there was only one age; it appeared to be one of a series,
but its followers were all parts of it. Bronze fell off to iron in the
chains of fable, and rose to steel in the technological degrees, but
gold, brass, pinchbeck and shoddy were all corners of the same room:
one could stand in one or another, but one was equally unwarmed
by the fading coals in the vast grate. This was the time and place of
where we still are and probably will be, and it is hard to tell whether
one is better off knowing this or not.

IV

And then? Even if we imagined some
Entirely different kind of time, or place
For whatever would happen next to fiddle
With—even if unimaginable
Phases in the prolonged existences
Of such barely imaginable things
As our lust for exemplifying might
Cause us to strain for were at hand to build
A last age from, the whole thing would collapse
Into the rubble of the third again.
It would be like the wings toward which a sad
Vaudeville clown would turn for respite, only
To find himself bounced back on stage once more.
A kind of negative apocalypse
Keeps ruining not what has gone before
But what would stand for everything to come
After the paling series of befores.
Almost as if the treasure of a last
Time, a final place, where to be guarded
As jealously as an origination,
Or a vacuum-surrounded metal metre
Kept in a bureau of eternal standards.
But it is not that "And so, we are back
Where we started from"; rather, we have come
To an understanding of the age we have
And will have, of the sense of an unending
That, given our own ends, we settle for
As easily as into a firm chair
At a clear table with an empty page
Beginning to wrinkle already now
Its wide brow, puzzled by our moving hand
What it will do and what it will not do—
But yielding up its blank simplicity.

A GARDEN IN PASADENA

Cantus: the faintest and perhaps the most distant birds,
    Answered in alto by the active
Modulations of others, both obstinately
    Shrill and fluent, here among roses
And olives, cypress, eucalyptus, palm and pine—
    A natural figure of open
Space unenclosed by walls, but hedged around by old
    Meanings that we plant about gardens,
A figure of place as it is inherent in
    Space's very possibilities.

This is where the music is, where lower voices
    Bear flourishing melody above,
Not sounds as of some gods, dropping in on this place
    To see what all the peace was about,
But Californians in their plain, unvarnished cars
    Buzzing by, parallel with power
Mowers trimming away at the tedious green
    Growth of grass. Such droning vehicles,
Themselves the tenors of a chorus of meanings,
    Move through a demesne more general
Than this open hall in which their voices become
    Parts of song—that unamenable
World without the walls even of narrow margins
    Hedging the pages of choiring texts.
They move through an implacable mist, through hazy
    Hills, Mount Wilson unobservable
Above and beyond, between desert and ocean.
    That unbounded space only resounds
With the basest voice coming from the highest source—
    Rumbling in a long phrase of thunder,
An eastward jet, retreating from the Old Idea
    Of Openness Westward, promised space.

And so it is this place, placed here as if in some
    Midst—between two ancient rivers, or
Walled in among the outside walls of rooms where most
    Of life goes on—it is this place which
Is the nest of consciousness where the songbirds weave
    Their birdsong among lower voices.
Flowering trees, perennial anthologies
    Of the outcry of color against
Versions of green, calculated plots of bright shrubs
    Empebbled, flowers of rhetoric
Blaring the brightest colors of unburning fire—
    All these compose themselves in evening
Calm, even at noon, or soon after. When the light
    Has weight, and when the undimmed music
Still taking place here comes to a consonant sigh,
    Wind roughs up the grass, and petals shake.
Then brisk bands of shadows, dropping in on this place
    To see what all the space was about,
Give over their chattering locus to insects,
    Birds and leaves, and become absorbed in
Turf as if it, finally, were the element,
    Dark and heavy and soundlessly deep,
Which bore this light, these voices, and their images
    Of pleasance and flight, and all the rest.

INSTRUCTIONS TO THE LANDSCAPER

I

You must have the Garden respond to all seasons by showing, in its aspects, significant versions of the meaningless blossoming, the cold, grave slumber, the fall and all that, versions of what is happening to what generally grows at these latitudes.

II

At the entrance, one must be made to pass through a representation of the whole Garden, but so placed that it is only while leaving it all, deliciously wearied by walking in the heats and shades, that one sees the entrance again in the new light of what it had always stood for—as if to have given a point to exiting.

III

Of the carved fountains, placed wherever they are to be at the centers of open spaces, or up at one end of them, at least one must be shaped in an antique myth of Eloquence, and at least one must embody a fable of Helplessness. In neither case, then, will they look contrived.

IV

There must be a stream, and a winding, ascending path along a slight rise that crosses and recrosses the stream on tiny stone bridges several times, vanishing into rocks and foliage in between the crossings. This is in order that, when one emerges from a state of shadow into a sudden openness, a wide glance around cannot fail to include a glimpse of where one had already been, at an earlier time, heading unthinkingly into the more recent darkness.

V

If there are to be ornamental gates representing Virtues, paths of ancient Rightness, temples to the spirits of time and place, then let each one, half-hidden from many viewpoints in the luxuriance of green, afford a prospect of one of the others: from one side of the rounded Temple of Honor, for example, it is appropriate that one should see, perfectly framed by two of the fluted columns, huddling in the rocks by the long water, the Grotto of Fear.

VI

In our climate, one may be plagued by hordes of starlings, and some recommend heroic measures against them. If they do gather, roosting nastily at sundown in the pine grove, making the needly floor stink with their droppings and the damp air shrill with their squawks, then wait, so they say, until a day when one's garden is closed to visitors. Torture one of the wretched creatures, we are told; record its woeful cries on a recirculating tape, and play it back continuously through small loudspeakers in the echoing grove: the others will all depart. But do not do this. Starlings will avoid the well-tended garden in any case. If they do come, you must abandon the whole place, for everything else will, in fact, have failed as well.

VII

If the Garden has been properly laid out, there need not be a maze in it. For the quest, the puzzlement, the contingency of the place of rest with its bench and rosebushes in the center of it all, the ease of entrance and its welcoming entrapment, the problems of homing, will all have been provided by the Garden itself. And the maze's parable, unrolling beneath the hurrying feet of the last wanderers on a summer evening that now chills and darkens—the parable of how there can be no clarity of truth without puzzlement, no joy without losing one's way—will be propounded by the Garden's final perfection, namely, that in it is no trace of the designer, that no image of him can ever be found. He—you—will have disappeared into the ground of the place that had been made.

THE TRIMMER

Long after the lone mower has
Gone by, the hidden sickle-bar
Hissing unheard beneath the
Mutter of his witty engine
Making mock of all gardening,
I come in the late afternoon
To do what's left to do in the
Penultimate light, the Trimmer.

With straight, unpainted clippers and a skilled, caressing shaping
hand I lop away until the hedge itself becomes the merest edge of a
lawn so long overgrown it has no boundaries of its own, but needs
the topiary grace of green walls to remain a place.

Gardeners bet on green: with me
All bets are hedged, color put down
In black and white, and most high hopes
Are pruned, that a few may flourish.
Cutting back and shaping up, late
In the day, I move among still
Leaves and unwhispering shadows:
My breath, my clippers speak for them.

—Even as they go clattering against the late results of spring and
early summer, come to grief in this exuberance of leaf. The low
sun shears my shadow slim, keeping me more and more in trim and
putting, as it gently slips downward, my clippers in eclipse.

I have beaten scythes into my
Shears, ploughshares into my chainsaw,
To war not on excess, but on
The choking ramifications
Of the literal. What nature
Shaped into wilderness became
The stony fate of gardens forced
Into green incivility.

With quaint-sounding trochaic-snips, caressing archly-rounded hips
and flanks of well-cut animals and urns, I summon up each shape
that turns out not (as the fable goes) to be embedded in repose within
the shapelessness of shrub, but in the mind's own green hubbub.

> Above those obvious plots and
> Schemes of planting, the sun passes
> Behind thick bushes of cloud from
> Time to time, summoning up
> Dark forms of shadow on the grass
> That is now greener and colder.
> Forms that inhere neither in sun
> Nor cloud, nor yet in the dark ground.

The thin curve of a weakened moon, hung high above the afternoon
merits my merest random glance, pale in its insignificance though
colored momentarily by twilight fear, it looks to be the hammered,
red sickle, or far-reaching green, crescent scimitar.

> Yet when all is said and done, the
> Reflections of green in other
> Greens, the unfolding history
> Of shaped versions of shapelessness
> Imaged later on in contrived
> Wilds come down to this evening trim,
> Each opening of shears a breath
> Of meaning, our hedge against death.

MORE QUATRAINS FROM HARP LAKE

The thrumming waves of the lost lake had gone
  Into some kind of hiding since the spring.
His long yawn ceased to deafen, then switched on
  The sixty-cycle hum of everything.

» «

Once we plucked ripened fruit and blossoms all
  Together from one branch, humming one note.
Spring from the water, shining fish, then fall
  In one unbroken motion into my boat!

» «

The river whistled and the forest sang,
  Surprised, then pleased, that something had gone wrong.
The touches of your hands, your silence, rang
  Changes on the dull, joyous bells of song.

» «

They stood tall, loving in the shade; the sunny
  Air withdrew from them in a sudden hush.
The strong-arm tactics of the oak? The honey-
  Dipped diplomacies of the lilac bush?

» «

In from the cold, her reddened ears were burning
  With what the firelight had been saying of her.
This final urn is wordless now, concerning
  Her ashes and the ashes of her lover.

» «

Under their phrases meaninglessness churned;
   Imprisoned in their whispers lay a yell.
Down here we contemplate the deftly-turned
   Newel-posts of the stairway up to hell.

» «

High on the rocks some Ponderosa pine
   Must overlook the jagged valley's floor.
What then must one have witnessed to divine
   That death was just a side effect of war?

» «

He'd long since put his feet into that part
   Of life from which they could not be withdrawn.
Late blossoms danced, then shook and took to heart
   Summer's long shadows falling on the lawn.

» «

Words of pure winter, yet not pinched nor mean:
   Blue truth can handle a good deal of gray.
Dulled, but incontrovertibly still green,
   The noble laurel holds the cold at bay.

AT A FOREST POOL

Here sad self-lovers saw in tragic error
Some lovely other or another sky;
In your reversing yet unlying mirror
I saw I was I.

ONTOLOGY IS A MATTER
OF MIDNIGHT

Now in the moonlight with which we mind the world
Horsebuns, kicked-up dust and pale bedraggled
Goldenrod are the August occasions, and
We never stop to botanize among our
Own ramified tangles of botanizing,
Let alone crash through the thicket and out toward
The blue of being in the sky, clouded or
Not. Take your flashlight and blanket out into
The meadow, Martin, and take your time: we shall
Have gone inside, who sat so long in the high
Twilight, cracking nuts and pelting the boulders
With shells, and in between whiles regarding the
World, that had been full of meanings all day long,
Flamboyantly turning the tables on what
Was true of it, until just before darkness
Finally came on, all the day's dismemberments
Fused into a recollection, melted and sank, and
All meanings became for a while full of the world,
And light and dark lay embracing in the grass.

MORNING IN THE ISLANDS

We had sat up all night hearing it roar, the mere
Sea, roaring out of the large darkness that was full
Of the only idea of ocean, overarched
Higher above our listening than what we heard
Was itself above the roaring. Then afterwards,
Day came toward us wearing an argument of light:
It turned us to the brightness of our deceptions,
The rightness of our wrongings of the visible
Sky, in all its various state of mind. It was
To get the point of some pediment, supported
By studied columns above a deeply read sea,
That we ourselves had kept on being part of the
Picture for so long. Behind us, intent on far
Distances, were clear-headed cliffs; below, what we
Had been ignoring sang in the heart of the rock.

HUSH!

A touch of the hand—say, of my forefinger
To your lips, not cautioning as you might me,
But quietly exemplary—can give all
But voice to silence without breaking it.
For such shades of vocation I could give over
The otium of the oatstraw filled with breath,
The evening whistling in the Dixie of
Solitude; I would study those solaces
As if deaf, becoming a philosopher
In my fifth and fiftieth year, a stopped pipe
That knows its own wind, an unheeding reed
Plucked from its place beside the mirroring pond
Unruffled, blown by gusts of mind that give
All but touch to surface. I would hang
The heart of music on the willing limb
Of this or that undreaming tree that stands
Beside the water without having that matter,
Without need of more than the peace of its own place.

MARKS AND NOISES

Potters, in the stark childhood of our writing,
Scratched the bent letters they could hardly use
As the shadows of voice yet over their cups
And urns for decorative purposes.
Long afterwards, abandoned alphabets
Which could not stand for language any more,
The disused runes, the dark, square Hebrew letters
Adrift in Christendom, shriveled to mere
Magic, and long since silenced hieroglyphs
Faded into pictures of mysteries.
O letters! O domestic ghosts! the spectres
Of dead speech, they rise up about me now
From stillborn sounds laid out on this lined sheet.
O sounds of the darkened sky! Far across Long
Island Sound and its thrum of winds and waters
There drift toward me ghosts of the ancient dead
Sight of you, standing long once in your hair.

ADDING A DASH OF INFERENCE

The curved bowl of a soupspoon lying here
On the bare counter colors with a flash
Of momentary false intelligence
As we happen to catch sight of ourselves
Chopping vegetables by the kitchen window.
(If perhaps not sight of ourselves exactly,
Then of the traces of light left somewhere
By the motions of our work, if only of
A moving head, or a brushing away
Of something that has finally been dealt with.)
But what other sort of knowledge is it that
The soupspoon cannot share, cannot hold back
Even a suspicion of? Ah, that red point
Of light informing us that the oven is hot—
It keeps the best of what it knows a sharp
Secret, constant and always blind to us.
Yet it is dull of spirit, credible,
And much less useful than the mindless soupspoon.
(But this is between us and the kitchen window.)

TO A SCULPTOR

(An Essay on the Origin and Nature of Relief)

A potter from a town near Corinth had
A daughter—(matters that now drive you mad:
Giving relief to the flat pain of stone,
Awakening its surface to the tone
Of an alarming chisel-blow that brings
Dream and depth to it while the metal rings;
Pushing flat fiction and its unreal space
Farther away from some slab's vacant face,
Farther away, and yet not having hacked
Out through the back, to the dull light of fact;
Urging forms to come forward from the cave
You'd cut them into; being still the slave
To the intransigency of the stone
You're master of—from her, almost alone,
The potter's daughter in antiquity,
These all stem.) *"How?"* you say? Read on and see.

A daughter, then. To say "a spirited
Girl" in the weak, old way of now-unread
Novels, might put it well: a breath of light
Suffused her, and enraptured Pliny quite
When he recounted how the girl was taken
With love of a young man and, quite unshaken
On hearing that he had to go away
On business overseas, resolved to stay
At home—with more of him, it seems, than just
Ashes of absence and desire's dust.
We might shade in the space the outline of
The old account leaves blank: did she say, "Love,
Don't leave me. Hold me. I'll hold you somehow,
Even after you've gone. Gone even now,
Somehow's some part of you: more shadowy,
The part of you that's still here"? If so, he
Protested. But her eyes flickered and gleamed

With more than mirrored light—it must have seemed
To him—and more than tears. "A shadow's all
I'll hold," she said, and outlined on the wall
With steady brush and eyes no longer damp
The shadow of his face thrown by the lamp
("Umbram et facie eius ad lucernam,"
Says Pliny) as if thereby to intern him,
Or something of him, in depiction's vast,
Totally flattened room. Not just his cast
Shadow, which in some fairy-tale she might
Have clapped into a box, not just the light
That darkest shading sheds on the dull blank
Of emptily-lit surfaces, but—thank
Euskia, Muse of Drawing!—what her brush
Left on the wall spoke louder than the hush
Of absence when, next day, he'd gone; it had
Far more enduring substance than his sad
And fleeting shadow, whose shadow she drew,
Thrown not by the blind lamp, but by the true
Light of her own eye. Far more like his face
Than the poor silhouette, the shadow's trace
Remained true of his soul, aside from merely
Projecting what the dumb lamp all too clearly
Had to say of one aspect of him. (Plato,
Remember, hints that even a potato
Is a mere image of Potatohood
Which, with the True, the Beautiful, the Good
And various other capitalized nouns,
Dwells in the heights of being. Plato frowns
On objects, as on aspects of them, and
—Though painted by the most imposing hand—
On views of aspects of shadows of the real.
But let Plato alone, who cannot deal
With images that shadow forth true forms
Directly, with a fire that lights and warms
The eye and heart and whispers to the mind.
Let reason's insight stay forever blind.)

—"*But this*, you say, "*is just another fiction*
About the primal moment of depiction,
An old Greek story, like the one about
The man who first traced his own shadow out
Along the ground, Narcissus-like, at noon
(Not in the shady lighting of the moon,
All the more feigning for remaining fainter,
Who, in herself, was truly the First Painter).
This story's just like that, save that desire,
Longing, not self-absorption lit the fire
Of first mimesis. Well. All this we know.
Get to the point. You always wander so."—

And you? You never let me finish. For
The point—her father was a potter; more
Out of some sense that images must face
You out of the convex or the concave space
They need to breathe in (so a potter might
Have to feel)—more from this than from some slight
Regret for his daughter's having to make do
With shadowy tracings without substance, threw
Some clay against the wall, inside the line
Of image she had drawn, and by design
(Not, as Frost says, "of darkness to appall"
But more of thickness to break up the wall)
Pressed it in, pushed, pulled, modelled—to be brief
(At last, I know) he made the first relief.

"*Relief?*" From flatness, as I promised you:
Lifting up ground from its dull page into
The realms of figure, raising from the dead
The ghosts of distance from their stony bed.
Fiction of picture, lying fact of mass:
Between them, a thin corridor, to pass
Along which is to move in lonely places
Unfilled with figures simpering on their bases,
Cut-ups nastily papering the walls,
Twiddled-with rods, or deconstructed balls,

Domestic playthings for mad dolls, and scary
Piles of dull beam and board that statuary
Has sunk into in its last, literal phase.
The regions where you spend your working days
Are places of whose pregnant emptiness
You know too well and I can only guess,
Lit by the chisel, carved by what the pen
Shades rumors of. Well! Save for nine or ten
More points about how images unfold
Their inner worlds by being not too bold
With roundedness, I've told—if not in brief,
At least in truth—the Fable of Relief
And moralized it, for your delectation,
With commentaries about figuration,
Literalness, absence and presence, and
High matters of the eye and of the hand
I've spent ten dozen lines on, more or less.

—"Then may I please get back to work now?   Yes.

SAUL STEINBERG, *untitled drawing*

Collection of the artist; by permission

34

AVE AUT VALE*

Are they standing in expectant greeting?
In innocent, unsuspecting goodbye?
'*Ah, no, the years, the years . . .*' While their image
Was being taken from the only life
They had, it was hard—wherever we were
At that time ourselves—not to take umbrage
At the way in which the shadows of all
Our lives kept falling across the very
Forms of those lives—shadows falling along
Doorsteps, reddened sands, desirable thighs,
Sighing water, responsive emulsions.
It was hard not to find unbearable
The way the images had been preserved:
Not that method in itself but for the
Mortality of the momentary
Models. And for the rush of time in which
Each pebble of bright hail is already
Melting into grayish floods of farewell.

* "Either hail or farewell"

CLAUDE MONET, *La route de la ferme St-Siméon*, Honfleur, about 1867

Courtesy of The Harvard University Art Museums (Fogg Art Museum);
Grenville L. Winthrop bequest

36

EFFET DE NEIGE

FOR ANDREW FORGE

SAYING:

Figures of light and dark, these two are walking
The winter road from the St. Simeon farm
Toward something that the world is pointing toward
At the white place of the road's vanishing
Between the vertex that the far-lit gray
Of tree-dividing sky finally comes down to
And the wide arrowhead the road itself
Comes up with as a means to its own end.
Père and Mère Chose could be in conversation
Or else, like us, sunk into some long gaze
Unreadable from behind—they are well down
The road, but not yet far enough ahead
For any part of them we can make out
To have been claimed by what we see of what
They move against, or through, or by, or toward.
Toward ... that seems to be the whispered question
That images of roads, whether composed
By the design of our own silent eyes
Or by the loud hand of painting, always puts.
Where does this all end? What is the vanishing
Point, after all, when finally one reaches
The ordinary, wide scene which begins
To reach out into its own vanishing
From there. Toward ...

SEEING:

:   :   :   :   :

SAYING:

Yes. You'd want that said, (if you
Want anything said at all, which I still doubt)
—The place the road ends, that patch of white paint
Marked with a dark stroke from the left, encroached

Upon from the right by far trees, that white place
Sits at the limit of a kind of world
That only you and I can know. Les deux
Choses, Mère and Père, undreaming even of fields
Of meaning like these—the world created by
That square—Oh, 56 x 56
Centimeters—that the height of the canvas
Cuts out of its width (81). Unfair
To mark that square, perhaps: were Mère and Père
Chose to walk out of it, they'd have to pass
Out of the picture of life, as it were, out
Through the back of the picture at the patch of white
At the end of the road. Even if they are staring
Down the long course of the gray slush of things
How can they get the point of how a world
Like theirs ends? From what distant point of vision
Would their world not remain comfortably
Coextensive with everything? How could they know?
What can we know of whatever picture-plane
Against which we have been projected? What ...

SEEING:

:   :   :   :   :

SAYING:

Oh, I know. The snow. The effective snow
Of observation lying on the ground
Given by nature will soak into it.
Wheel tracks entrench themselves in snow, yet painted
Traces of those deep cuts lie thickly upon
The high whites spread over the buried earth.
Shadows keep piling up as surfaces
Are muffled into silence that refuses
To pick up even the quickening of wind
In dense bare branches, or the ubiquitous
Snaps of ice cracking in the hidden air.
Silence. Your way of being. Your way of seeing
Still has to be intoned, as in a lonely

Place of absorbing snow, itself to be
Seen. What you know is only manifest
When I am heard, and what I say is solely
A matter of getting all that right . . .

SEEING:

:   :   :   :   :

SAYING:

I know,
I've drifted somewhat from the distant heart
Of the matter of snow here. Both of us have grasped
That patch of white at the very end of the road
As it sits there like an eventual
Sphinx of questioning substance, or a sort
Of Boyg of Normandy . . .

SEEING:

:   :   :   :   :

SAYING:

Yes. The obvious
Standing in the way of the truth. A white
Close at the end of distance the two Chose
People might see to be the opening
Out of the road into a way across
Wide, whited fields, a way unframed at last
By trees—or might see as the masonry
Of a far barn, just where the road curves sharply
Right, and appears from here to be overcome
By what it seems to have moved toward. In any
Event, the end of the painted road ends up
In white, in paint too representative
Of too much truth to do much more than lie
High on this surface, guarding the edge of Père
And Mère Chose's square of world, even as they
—Now that you notice it—have just moved past
The edge of that other square cut from the right

Side of the painting, the world of that wise, white,
Silent patch of ultimate paint. You are
Grateful, I know, for just such compensations,
That neither the motionless farm couple trudging
Toward the still dab of white that oscillates
From point to point of meaning—open? closed?—
Nor, indeed, the bit of paint itself can know of.

SEEING:

:   :   :   :   :

SAYING:

Mère and Père Chose are walking away from the
Two of us, Docteur and Madame Machin, who stand
Away from their profundity of surface.

SEEING:

:   :   :   :   :

SAYING:

The truth, blocking the path of the obvious.

BAIGNEUSE

(By Jules Scalbert, Salon de 1912, According to a Postcard)

Like some exquisite afterthought she lingers
Froward, as if the stream nearby had taught her
Half-stillness, and had shown evasion to her
Body of water

Lying along its bank in waves of light and
Deep shade that tells truly of caves and hollows
Of solace in bright hills; the light-splashed eye then
Leads to what follows

Beyond the musing sepias of faintly
Naughty postal cards like part of the river
Not shown in the picture. But near her knee the
Flickering quiver

Of old nostalgic light on the bit of water
Calls up caverns it has wandered inside of
(Below one of the rocks this slow stream now steers
Warily wide of).

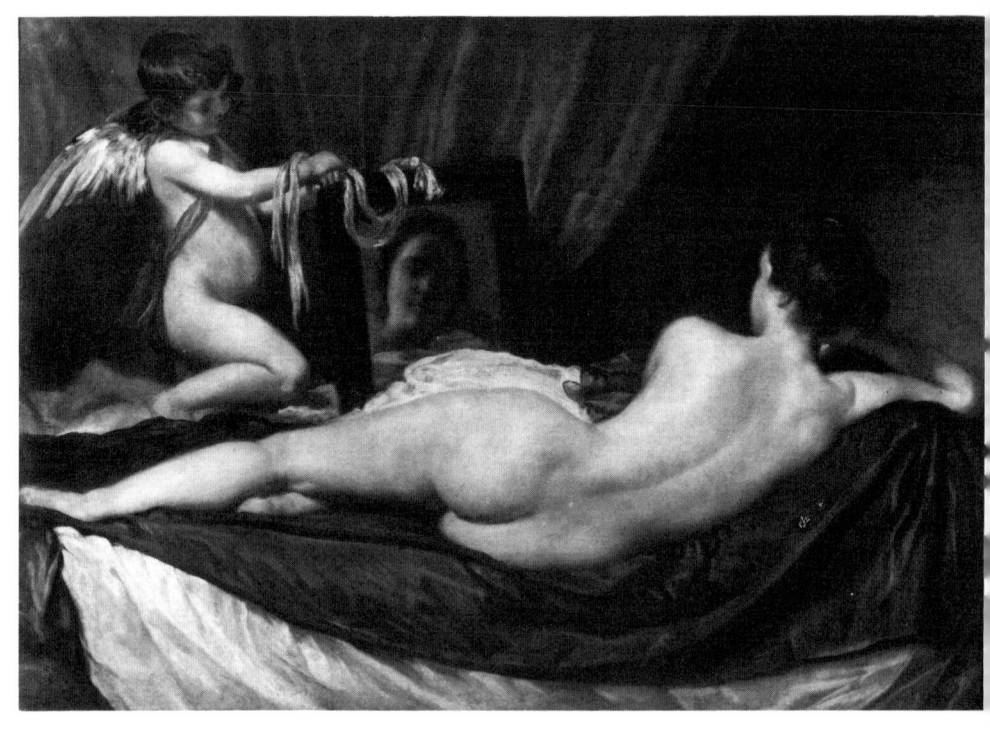

VELÁZQUEZ, *The Rokeby Venus*

London, National Gallery; courtesy of Marburg/Art Resources, New York

42

TO THE ROKEBY VENUS

One need not (and I say this without malice)
   Be one of those who hate
The thought of entering a lovely palace
   Save by the postern gate,

To gaze so deeply at you, Goddess, turned
   Away now to confront
Yourself, trembling Adonis for whom you burned
   Long since dead in the hunt.

Unseen by yours, our eyes are open to
   Unclouded perfect grace;
Your meditative son holds up to view
   The true, the mirrored face.

Mars, Vulcan and Anchises in their kind
   Each had you in his day;
Velázquez gazing at you from behind
   Saw more of you than they.

```
          I        a
        cat      who
        coated in a
        dense shadow
        which I cast
        along myself
         absorb the
          light you
         gaze at me
        with can yet
        look at a king
        and not be seen
        to be seeing any
       more than himself
      a motionless seer
        sovereign of gray
       mirrored invisibly
      in the seeing glass
     of air Whatever I am
     seeing is part of me
     As you see me now my
     vision is wrapped in
     two green hypotheses
       darkness blossoming
        in two unseen eyes
         which pretend to be
           intent on a spot of                    bug
            upon
             the
             rug
           Who
           can
            see
              how
                eye
                  can
               know
```

AN OLD ENGRAVING

The one-year-old baby is crawling among skulls,
   Eye-sockets handled, rounded cranium
Cradled in two fat arms: the hollowness of bone
   Makes light of mortality and its weight.
An infant hand can move a skull, yet cannot budge
   A full head, can sport in the bony holes
But could not bear the contained heaviness of thought.
   Which of these is toying with the other—
The child, with unread emblems it will grow into
   Knowing? The wise old image, with its doll?
At our dear, silly games we are the playthings of
   Bone dice we don't know that we've betted on.

INSCRIBED ON A SHARD OF
HOUSEHOLD (?) POTTERY

(*from the Archaic*)

Why am I given to speak for what once was whole?
  The other fractured half pleads only for
Herself, as if because of having been broken
  Off, as if in outcry of jaggedness.
Together we held more than air . . .
  . . be cradled . . . . .
How can something entire be cracked in two leaving
  A broken edge on only the one piece?

THANKS FOR A BOTTLE

Dear Angus: We broke out tonight
In the unconcentrated light
Of eight black candles (lamps of hell?)
Your lovely bottle of Beychevelle,
Sprung and fallen, reaped and conceived
In the same gentle, many-leaved
Summer of nineteen sixty-seven
(My thirty-eighth quick year to heaven).
It tasted of its family tree
And chemical biography
In vine, in wood and in—alas—
Its veritable gaol of glass
—Not of that past year of its birth
When I lay on the grass-rich earth
Beside the trivial, moving Cam,
Unbuilding me toward what I am,
—Not of the ravages and tears
Of seven intervening years
That helped unbuild a world of hope
To its decaying isotope:
The history of this dark wine
Is, thankfully, untouched by mine.
But as the candles gutter out,
The bottle emptied beyond doubt
Down to its common sediment
We wonder, breathless, where it went,
The claret of our middling years
Remembered; as it disappears,
Inside the green glass shadows fall.
It is dark. Emptiness is all
Toward which we stare with eyes yet bright
That make a little, glooming light,
Recalling, just before the end
(As the last breaths of flame descend)
The gift, the giver and the friend.

THE WIDENER BURYING-GROUND

In spite of all the learned have said,
We hear the voices of the dead.
Not scholiasts who like Burke and Hare
Turn dead leaves in the living air,
Unlock the Essay and exhume
Philosophy from its dry tomb,
Nor wise embalmers of the text
In humble buckram or perplexed,
Carved, interlaced half-calf, who come
To show how gold they are, and dumb—
We strike from silent lines a fire.
Troped sea-shell, loud Aeolian liar,
Nymph-haunted cave and mountain-peak
Choir with voices that we seek
As, scholars of one candle-end
We hear the hush of dusk descend.
We unfired vessels of the day,
Built of a soft, unechoing clay,
Grow obdurate of ear at night
When images of voice are bright:
The dreamingale, the waterlark,
Within the present, silent dark
Echo the burden (on these stairs
Mistranslated) the singer bears—
He who packs, with a glowing faith,
In that portmanteau, fame and death.
Our marginalia all insist
—Beating the page as with a fist
Against a silent headstone—that
The dead whom we are shouting at,
Though silent to us now, have spoken
Through us, their stony stillness broken

By our outcry (*we are the dead*
Resounding voices in our stead)
Until they strike in us, once more,
Whispers of their receding shore,
And Reason's self must bend the ear
To echoes and allusions here.

FOR A TALL HEADSTONE

"I told you I was sick!"

EPITAPH IN A FLORIDA CEMETERY

No, it was I who never listened
  To myself
While the brazen clock that glistened
  On the shelf
Ticked away at the horizon
  Of my hearing.
The world is noise: my silence lies in
  A kind of clearing,
Yet in the failing light outside
  I should have hearkened
While inner twilight horrified
  My heart and darkened.
It was not that you never paid
  Enough attention
To everything I never said
  Or failed to mention:
No, it was yielding to that terror,
  Closing my eyes
Against the inconsiderate mirror
  Of unstarred skies,
Heeding it not. Now blind and dumb
  To you who pass—
Stone speaks for me—I have become
  That looking-glass.

LOOKING AHEAD

When afternoons appear brighter, making us forget
That it is not midday anymore, nor will be, then
May be the time to avert our eyes from the shining
Center of the field, from the famous ancillary
Groups on either side affirming that centrality,
And consider what had long been too close to the frame:
Mercury stirring up the broth of air at the edge
Of Botticelli's Spring, not to conjure up a swarm
Of golden honeying bees but to becloud the light
From above a little. Which may not be what we want,
But remains what we have to have, given everything:
The plain view of things being in a kind of shadow
Anyway, mirrors having lost their amazement, and
Paintings and photos otherwise occupied in still
Needed picturing of their own representative
Acts, we had better use what we have in the way of
Interpositions (clouds, fogging of the spectacles—
We all know of more). Otherwise we might easily
Move by imperceptible degrees toward rejecting
The one interim revision of what is clearly
There, that somehow lies at the bottom of all others—
And that shows us the dark, rounded mouth of the tunnel
Ahead, rather than the fact of the true opening,
Similar in diameter but more horribly
An exit, not an entrance: the fact of our being
In the tunnel now, not racing over the varied
Terrain, the distant mountains, the cultivated plain,
The patches of blue sea eying us from between hills
As we pass by but, even faster than we could gauge,
Hurtling on through the dark tube in which there is only
One direction, the way out. All this comes from looking
Ahead, seeing well what is there, and having to put
Something—in this case there are only our own eyes—in
The way of that final evening of all the odds.

THE SENSE OF UNENDING

FOR FRANK KERMODE

In the shortness of breath,
In the breadth of the night,
In the middle of bright
Islands far from the white
Intimations of death
In our shivering clime,
In the ending of light
There lie flashes of hope
Of a Final Sublime
For which death is a trope.

No. No general case
Of an End can erase
The too-literal mark
Of the crestfallen dark,
The horizon erect;
No Last Thing can deflect
The true, terrible flight
Of pain toward delight,

So that every life dies
With no comfort at all
In the thought that the skies
Will be cancelled, the eyes
Of the world be put out,
And a colorless pall
Cover darkness itself,
Yea, and brightness itself
Bleach away in a shout
Of revision. Such lies
As that All will ascend
At the end of the end
Are what tales are about.

No, it all will go on.
Only we will be gone.

It will always be now
When the books are unsealed,
When up, down, and how
Both are one, are revealed
As modes that depart
At each subsequent start.
Now Omega can rhyme
With her Aleph, embrace
Face to end, end to face,
First and last lost in slime;
As the sun sets in brass
Fallen kings feed on grass,
All is ice at the prime:
There is no kind of crime
That will not come to pass
In the foulness of time.

ON THE DEATH, TOO LATE IN SPRING, OF MY FIRST LOVE

The apple blossoms have been snowed upon.

(—*A one-line poem, or an unfinished one?*)

Who wrote that note? my life is none of his
Business, even if asking questions is.
My flowers freeze: their frozenness may flower
For years or fall, the flower of an hour.
(Signed, with a flourish I'm half weary of)
"On the Death, Too Late in Spring, of My First Love."

NEW GRAVEYARD IN NEW JERSEY

One stands almost grateful in the freezing air
To feel mildly alive, shovelling some earth
Into the broken ground while new fields lie all
Around, fallow, awaiting spring or summer
Plowings, or the jackhammers of deep winter
Again, to blossom sometime in white tombstones.
It is too cold and too late in the year to pluck
A handful of grass and mutter of grass and
Dust. Up toward the eastern horizon, the high-
Way—down toward the low, grayish hills westward—
Runs out in a broad, constantly extending
Band whose traffic even in this clear air sighs
Rather than roaring. The cold spade drops its dirt
Quietly into earth's dry, ungrateful trough.

A FOOTNOTE ON DESIGN

I had a black cup once, I had a black
Cat; the black cat from Manhattan broke
The black Etruscan cup; a car (Connecticut)
Broke the black cat. But even now, to assume
For purposes of—what? some X—that the unknown
Car was black, would make the question of just
What "X" could ever be appropriate here
Far too heavy for the frail decencies
Of mourning to bear. What black there was in fact
Mumbles its own tale of the shattering
Of repetition. And the words that were
Clear glass, through which you could see my well-lit
Meaning, have all become mirrors or worse.

ALL OUR POEMS OF DEATH
ARE JUVENILIA

The breaking of things can look like an origination
But then reveal itself, through lights shimmering in fragments
Of smashed glass, as having occurred too late to have given
Birth to anything but a lighting up of just how late
It was—So with a crystal night of crashings that might be
Taken to have started out all our present darkening,
Like a plumber's tools dropped into a box full of glass eyes,
Unretractable, the panes of fractured window, jagged,
Clear, looking down into black water and scarred cobblestones,
Looking out into where we are now, a confirmation,
Not an arrival. And yet our dry mouths thirst for the splash
Of some outset, some source, some once. We'll have, then, for a scene
To start with something from the end of the story, a room
In hospital, with walls the color of late afternoon.

Dr. Frank Heller lies there with the sun at his right hand
The opaque black lenses before his eyes pierced with a pair
Of tiny eyes through which he stares down the narrowing hall
Dark time has cut out of the years' colorless rock for him.
Nurse Noctifer will soon arrive with his bowl of nothing,
And rearrive with a different name in the morning
To bathe him in shadows as he lies stiffly holding up
His head so as not to shatter again his broken eyes.
A huge black fly buzzes about the cold October room:
His buzzings are a substance more enduring than he, and
More seemingly palpable. Dr. Frank Heller had palped
Internal darkness, and he lay unmindful of the fly,
Permanence lost like childhood so far back that even the
Time during which it disappeared itself was long since lost.

Living beside the sea was a thing of the past; looking
Toward water (as if ahead), an inadvertent glance backward.
Across the city Dr. Frank Heller saw gleamingly

Through his two pinholes some of the river that lay westward.
And he saw boats that glided by degrees out of the mind:
Short tugs across the water, long, heavy-laden barges
Conveying themselves as in the images of themselves,
Could only come to him as floats in some distant Triumph
Of Passage. The light hurt. And given the pain of the Dark
Thought, his mind mirrored over behind the bright, black glasses,
So that what his visitors saw in the light of the room
Was something of their own broken looking, and what he had
Seen was a fiction now only of what he had to say.
This was not the first scene of last looks between Dr. Frank
Heller and others, but others would not look like this one.

MONTDÉSIR

The climb: we go up and up in a winding way
Toward the peak, consuming resources we had brought
Along, used-up cans themselves becoming ballast
At those heights whereat even breath gets heavier.
This long way, whose very way of being a way
We had known so well that even its special
Surprises were no longer surprising—its course
Is less apparent to the heart than a detailed
Account of it might be, thus making the account
Itself a course. Ah well—at the top at last, we
Can drop the final burden of wanting to have
Been up there at all: it falls silently, faster
Than gravity could draw it, straight down the sheer peak
Into the low shadows from which we started out.

THE MEANING OF IT

What the moon espied going on
In among bedsheets, the sun saw
Happening in the exhausted
Fields, in the shadows of haystacks:
The same tumble of in and out.
And yet the sun interpreted
The squirming in the straw, the coarse
Breath in the cricket-twanging air,
As but a masque in mimetic
Honor of his marriage with the
Land. The bright moon, however, knew
That what transpired below the day's
Work, its frivolous and fruitful
Commerce with the humdrum earth, was
Taught in her cool seminary
Of darkened beds: what happened there
Lay at the heart of the matter.

DESIRES OF HERE AND THERE

We of the north, the soundless, beating part
Of the recumbent world, where the hearth has
Its reasons which the seasons cannot know,
Yearn for the palmy wind of the southwest.
The laughing yucca mocking our own green
Weeps still within at thoughts of water, of
Our massive rivers running toward the main.
The warm palm pines not for the cold itself
But for the consequences of the cold:
The difficulty of the very air
Where circumstance solidifies; the sky
Which dark, untousled firs keep pointing at;
White lakes breaking up, ice coldly giving
Slow, painless birth to its own watery mother;
And even what we dream among ourselves
By an unfathomable eastern shore,
Dreams of high summer from whose echoing rocks
We hail a seal as a far sail heels over.

A FIND

Early middle-late: it was still a time of
Night when seen and unseen embraced in corners;
Borrowed light lent out yet again had slipped from
        Shoulders of surface;

Light lay spilled below, as if brightness had been
Poured, and all the hollows of evening filled with
Variously substantive shadow. It was
        then that I saw her,

Coming out that night in her cloudy nightgown,
High above this pool in the woods in winter
By a long, white stone that the slowly melting
        Snow had uncovered,

Cynthia Wax-Wayne, ravishing debutante (the
Longing water strove every night to capture
Her across his surface but, getting flustered,
        Mussed up her image

—So the story goes). I had ended up there
After half an hour of distracted ambling
On a cold path fringing the late March forest,
        Looking at moonlight.

What I seemed to see, though, was your remembered
Shadow lying solidly there asleep, a
Sound mind buried deep in a silent body;
        Then I seemed not to,

And I wandered into a broader darkness,
Slowly groping hand-over-hand along a
Twisted rope of words, like the many tropes of
        Shady Odysseus,

Certain, anywhere on the way, of turning
All directions into a kind of homeward
So that where he was—but where *does* one, finally
   Find oneself? Hiding

Out in forest shadows of half-remembrance?
Marching down the boulevard in the morning?
Where is where? ambiguously the question
   Asks us another:

Where are we indeed in the course of finding
Out where we are at? and along what stony
Moonlit riverbed do we walk until our
   Vivid conviction—

That we are at home in our moving bodies,
That they are at home in their very motion,
That their motion dwells in coordinates which
   Open their arms to

Homing points of vision—has come upon us?
Here, tonight, years later, the wind has risen
High inside the pinnacles of the shaking
   Spruces, dispersing

All those *wheres* in gusts of despairing, *when, O
When?* But, old, outside now a wider moon is
Covering the ground with a whitened layer
   Like one of snowfall

Bare of any shadows save of the spruces,
Clear of any signals or hidden signs, the
Kind I always seem to have had a predi-
   lection for reading.

Here inside, my pen on this yellow paper
Traces its own forests to lose itself in.
Following its broken, sporadic path, I
    Seem to remember

Heading for a thought of you like a kind of
Home, its breathing hearth and its warm, familiar
Bed; I even envy the touching distance,
    Bending itself to

All your contours, closer to you than I could
Ever be back then, or could now be, ever,
Closer far than I who am now a shadow
    Cast by the lamplight.

LEAVES FROM AN ALMANAC

1

SOMETHING FOR THE FALL WIND

The fierce heat of the yapping dog-days chases
The black *cattivo tempo* of a cold
July: so much for summertime, whose space is
Filled with ending beginning to unfold.
Comforting me with pomes and drupes whose falling
Song comes down to a whispering in the grass,
I patch together scraps of the appalling
Year that I brought to such a scattered pass.
And even when some temperate September
Metes out the dark and daylight in her scales,
What has been worked the late wind will dismember:
Well, let him, teller of tall autumnal tales,
Hail the high town's tight avenues, and tell
Him bid the flagrant summer vales farewell.

2

OCTOBER'S END

The trees turn, finally, after the long
Extended summer, the late wind bending
    And readying for the shatter
       And for the fall

Of dense, high walls, of the leafage wherein
Even the old panther of the year starts
    His ninth life in the knowledge of
       Scattering light.

3
MOUNT NOVEMBER

> Presented here, amid
> These dim hills with new kinds of red—
>   Maples coldly flaming,
> A first few final messages
>   Scenting the clear, gray air—
> Someone is staring in the near
>   Distance toward some single
> Trees, newly risen in the glare,
>   A low nova ember
> Growing slowly into its chill,
>   Sunset color. Some tree,
> For instance? for shadow of some
>   Distant truth? or for a
> Glow of mirroring that may flare
>   Up in a brief moment,
> Close to the end, of antique bronze.

4
INDIAN SUMMER, 1975

> This late warmth, taking away more than it can ever give,
> Comes at a time of death; it throws a momentary, sick
> Glory about our eyes, and we see the ransacked branches,
> The leaves flung like wet paper bags underfoot, to be less
> Timely than ever. There is no comforting chill now in
> The gray air, no harmonizing gasp of wind, no old screed
> Of winter birds scrawled on bare sky. This is wrong, a sunny
> Fortnight, a bad, late poem by November governed by an
> Inadequate synecdoche of warming that stands for
> What is gone and cold as well as for what can burn and glow.
> Yet it is no text for the gatherer of examples,
> Errant among those branches, who says *elm* when he means *ash*,
> Or when it is meant for him to mean something like ash, when
> It all comes down to ash—elm, oak, birch, myrtle—anyway.

5

LONG AFTER THE END OF FALL

The dead tree at the edge of the orchard mourns
The ground from which the snow has since departed,
A man in black regarding some whiteness lost
In an old story, bearing listless witness
To what we make of what we make it see,
Standing off from the sleepers, the bare-branched
Others. Unlike them, spring will not relieve
With green this misery of distant vision.
The rotten, unsustaining windfalls, scattered
Underfoot, unreadable for the deep
Meanings that shade the surfaces of apples,
The flecked originals of all the fallen,
Stand in for us when dead trees can no more.
Death will bite into us now, one by one,
Like apples plucked that never should have been,
Like apples all that never were intended
To be devoured, but for admiring time
Only to study, only to regard
With such a deep absorption it could never
Remember to take up its fell work again.

6

END PAPERS

Cold seeds fall to the verdant earth
Remembering—unencumbered
With what will not be brought to birth—
How slowly summer climbed
Its round green hill,
And how the heat this year took chill.
Sweat froze, and cold ticking drops timed
The trembling weeks, and numbered
The sombre cassocked months; I see
Them fall, hear them hiss jealously:
"Young"

        "You lie!"

                "*Angst*"

                      "Remember?"

"*Disrober!*"

          "... nor ember ..."

                     (Dissembler!)"

And hear, oh, here,
The end of the year.

A GLIMPSE OF PROSERPINA

Clear, early mornings as I stride
Westward, the usual brick street
Grows meadow grass from its concrete:
The neighborhood turns countryside.

Huge structures hovering across
The river like excluding shades
Collapse into the Palisades;
The river burns away its dross.

If I went up a nearby hill
You would be there in sight, bent down
To gather flowers at the crown
Of my hill's twin against the sky;

We'd meet where, as in fields of wars
Forgotten, stones and daisies swarm,
Then turn back, arm in flowers in arm,
And bring them quietly indoors.

BY THE SOUND

Dawn rolled up slowly what the night unwound
And gulls shrieked violently just out of sight.
That was when I was living by the sound.

The silent water heard the light resound
From all its wriggling mirrors, as the bright
Dawn rolled up slowly what the night unwound.

Each morning had a riddle to expound;
The wrong winds would blow leftward to the right,
In those days I was living by the sound:

The dinghies sank, the large craft ran aground,
Desire leapt overboard, perhaps in fright.
Dawn rolled up slowly what the night unwound.

But seldom, in the morning's lost-and-found
Would something turn up that was free of blight.
In those days I was living by the sound

The sky contrived, whose water lay around
The place that I was dreaming by the light
(Dawn rolled up slowly), what the night unwound
In those days. I was living by the sound.

BY THE GULF

Off to the Gulf and hoping to have the time of our lives,
We found but the signs of fever there: the prostrate horizon,
Unable to drink of the distance, and only appearing at sundown,
In a clear condition of length, to show any strength at all.
And over the blue of the water, the sun from out of the desert,
Waging in daily rage a *jihad* against the inane
Or, holding the body of night, sinking to languorous slumber,
Allowed of no shadowy play, or the vanishing dance of transitions.
More and more then we read at the texts we had taken along—
Letters of palpable liars, memoirs of exiled queens,
Mysteries, guides to the local antiquities, till the tidal
Rise and fall, and the puzzling smudges of cloud, and the question
Of what the light was like, scribbled their learned comments
Over the endpapers, over all the available flyleaves,
Until we were left with this sort of touching but pointless notation:

When the Temple stood we feasted on the roasted meat of the altar,
Now, in the time of remembering, our joy is the warming wine. Or

"M'amour" sighs the thrush in May, recalled as a lower "Ma mort"
By the bird of oncoming autumn: Love calls to Love and Like
To Like, as the daughters of water sang out to the boy of the wood
Till he followed and fell in their arms, becoming one with the water.

Or, *Madame Mamamouchie's crystal sphere could show in its*
    shadows
Never the future, but only the hidden heart of the present:
Your face, smeared into distortion; the fragments of lamplight;
    Madame's
Ne'er-do-well nephew, a manic assassin, approaching behind you.

Mostly, we left them back on the sands, these books of remembrance,
Charming in their marginalia, inapplicable to ourselves,
There by the Gulf. Not wishing to be confined by example
Or to be left behind, fretting, in our hotel rooms

While all the others went off to observe the splendid events
And exclaim at the famous sites, we joined their daily excursions,
After all. That was it, at the Gulf; and then having the time
Of our lives and the space of our language to move in, we set out
  for home,
Toward which, we have been assured, our troublesome journeys are
  headed.

ISLAND POND

FOR JAMES MERRILL

We stand here at the edge, the clumped sedge dense
And dull between us and the radiant water,
Seeming bewildered, more than a little dense
To the wide clarity that can condense
Coolly on surfaces, out of the higher
Kinds of light rendered more rare or dense
By the artful, varying coincidence
Of kinds of cloud high above where we stand.
The muddy shore shifts below where we stand:
We grab at the infirm air—such accidents
Shift the light balance of weight, touch and sight
And jiggle the clear pool of what's in sight.

What trembles in the light: wide gaze? insight?
The medium of the air is not so dense
As that pale, watery wall the very sight
Of water builds. To give our thirsty sight
Its taste of boundary, its brink of water,
Spirits of vision laid out just this site:
Here, in the sea of all that's out of sight
Right now, an island of water, where higher
Thoughts alight threadlike, like light flies, like hier-
oglyphs themselves of something about sight:
Seeing inherent in the scene. They stand
For what is part of all on which they stand.

Even as we watch still, behind a stand
Of reeds, there rises from this light a sight
For soaring eyes, now that we understand
The radiance of our gaze that can withstand
Substantive ground and watery accidence
(Some of the medieval terms still stand)
For we can just make out, from where we stand,
A tiny island in this isle of water,

On our dry island impounded in wide water . . .
Widening is height: as from the cool grandstand
I once traced a white baseball rising higher
And (to put it so tiresomely) higher . . .

Is it unfair that knowing still rates higher
Than merely seeing? Waving the high stand-
ard of Truth about as if it were for hire,
Some higher-up in the official hier-
archy of vision, some inner oversight,
Directs its own adoring eyes toward higher
Reflections: *Raise me*, prays lower light to higher;
Dollink, the wave croons to the shore, *ledz dence*;
Chérie, whispers the wind, *forgo zese dense
Silent oueeds on ze verge for somesing 'igher.*
But these poor fools disperse, like light in water
Of the wide sea, the inescapable water.

It is not land we are left with, but water
(Once the fog dies in search of something higher)
Afire with sunrise, dry eyesight's firewater.
Awakening as if to Handel's *Water
Music*, we trust the ground on which we stand,
Less superficial, we are told, than water
—As if land were a narrator, and water
A personage in some tale we could cite,
Prometheus, perhaps, or Soames Forsyte
(Fragile, prophetic fictions still hold water)
In one great blaze, or flickering incidents.
But water drinks of the shore, and grows more dense.

Sightless surroundingness and I (more dense)
Stand here beside you, having shared your water.
Hierophants of low land and of higher
Water, we leave our vision here to stand
Dense, luminous, like all that we have in sight.

TO ELIZABETH BISHOP

Last week, in playing fast and loose
With the dense foliage of Larousse
I came across the French for "Moose"

—It was "*original*", of course
(As if that creature were the source
Of nightingale and wingèd horse,

Etcetera.) The gloss then bred
A herd of meanings in my head:
"Elan du Canada" it said.

This echoing footstep was so pat
About what you'd been getting at,
I stopped and left it all at that.

(OCTOBER, 1977)

—Or so it seemed: my erring eye,
Blurred with desire, went awry
By adding an unwonted "i"

—The word was "*orignal*", of course
(Just yesterday, I checked the source);
Now, with chagrin but less remorse

I write once more, three years too late
To reach you in the living state,
To try to set the matter straight.

What must I now make, then, of my
Finding a hidden, seeing "I"
In "*orignal*"? A kind of lie

Against French verity? a vision
Of lyric truth caught in collision
Between two consonants? Misprision

(As someone else has put it) of
The letter, so that we may love
The figure, flying high above?

Perhaps the "I" was a decree:
"In all Originality
Where once God was, let ego be."

Or was it that I overheard
—Or thought I did—an antlered word
Of Frost's: not one about a bird

But in this case, about a male
Buck, crashing out once through frail
Underbrush to frame a tale

Of "counter-love, original
Response" (he thus meant echo, full
Of later sound, accountable

As much to what it makes of what
It's given, as to that it's not
The first voice, from the prior spot.)

But then, I must have been in doubt
As to what echoes are about:
If a buck answers to a shout

So a she-moose can make response
To echoing buck, for wisdom wants
Nothing called up just for the nonce.

So now, although I couldn't quite
Hope to put the whole matter right,
I've burned the extra "i" for light;

(And anyway, the other pun
—Your *élan*, once Canadian,
Now all of ours—found out in fun,

Retailed in awe, remains OK,
The wordwork of semantic play.)
That's that. I'm calling it a day.

BALLADE FOR RICHARD WILBUR

and, thereby, for the Duke of Orléans, who offered a prize at Blois, circa 1457, for the best ballade employing the line "*Je meurs de soif auprès de la fontaine*," won belatedly by Richard Wilbur with his poem with the refrain "*I die of thirst, here at the fountain-side*."

Eagles wheel by the crags where lizards crawl,
Castalia bubbles down the mountainside,
But here, beside the darkened city-wall,
The Genius of the Fountain's dreaded bride,
Smiling, green-eyed, slim-hipped and velvet-thighed,
Spoons up from somewhere in her hidden den
The poisoned waters with which all are plied.
Je meurs de soif auprès de la fontaine.

De la fontaine . . . the phrase seems to recall
The founts where wisdom spoke to please and guide:
The antic cicada fell dumb in the fall,
The crowing fox was smitten in his pride—
Fables whose faith our novels have denied
Rhyme in inevitable French again.
Athirst for truth where morals multiplied,
Je meurs de soif auprès de La Fontaine.

Young David's meanings struck the maddened Saul
With something more than music, and he died.
Rain from the palace courtyard fills the hall,
Drips into cups where disused shadows hide . . .
Something is rotten in the countryside
Within our sorrows and beyond our ken:
Ills are a deluge, yet our wells have dried.
Je meurs de soif auprès de la fontaine.

Dick (au lieu du Duc) I have never vied
With you for any prize; yet we're tied, for when
You "die of thirst, here at the fountain-side,"
Je meurs de soif auprès de la fontaine.

A THING SO SMALL

One of those dark butterflies called a Mourning
Cloak clung to a trumpet of morning glory,
Draping it with something of afternoon, a
      Palpable shadow

Flighty time itself would have never flung there
Just to trap me into interpretation,
One more unintentional emblem nature
      Seemed to have flashed one.

Like a firefly clapped in between two palms to
Keep its chilly signal alive and steady
Only after death, that can play the role of
      Simpleton Symbol

In the garden's theater of moralizing,
So the pointed syntax of the alighted
Flutterer atop the attentive flower
      Told an old story.

It was far too late in the day to think that
Some sharp arbitrator of settlements had
Known the name of butterfly and of flower
      And, for an hour,

Played with them and planted the somber insect's
Name in blue—a dawning of darkness—just as
If there were a species of creature labeled
      Paronomasia.

Still, the moment's prescience—the blue of evening
Sky the morning glory was drenched in, and the
Midnight purple of the unmeaning wings—had
      Wrapped me in wonder.

Then a random wind stirred across the vine and
Tugged at the meandering butterfly the
Passing of an instant had slapped against it.
            Holding and trembling,

My once dearest, holding and trembling—these are
Hard, clear, present matters of fact my silent
Heart starts up at; trembling, my tired knowledge
            Mutters of love my

Blinded, lame remembrance keeps slowly moving
Toward: for which of us was the flower of the
Day, and which the sorrowful traveler? We
            Trembled together

Through bright evenings, lay in the shadowed mornings,
Parting in the graying of afternoons while
Bells a mile away in the wind were sounding,
            Distantly clinging.

After twenty years then the opened flower
Shrugged at last, and suddenly dark unfolding
Wings made off with all that their vivid image
            Mapped on the past, and

There lay grass, unpressed by another presence,
There rose, fence-propped, only an ordinary
Morning glory vine. I was left with nothing
            More than the fading

Morning hour; my easy distrust of signs, that
Touching thoughts had stupidly clapped in irons;
My desire, that memory was intelli-
            gently caressing.

POINT OF ORIGIN

I can live now with concentricities
Neither in a dread nor an excitement
Both outgrown, like images that frightened
Me in childhood—anatomies, the Sphinx,
And, for yet one more example, pictures
—And here circles become their own analogues—
Of boring atoms in the paradigms
That physics can't be taught with any more.
Electrons seeming far too planetary
Terrified me with the spectre of scale:
Where were we? what were we? and what if the earth
Were an electron round some nuclear sun
In the galactic vastness of some smear
Of substance, say, the ink of that last dot
Of question-mark at the end of the schoolbook page?

But I grew out of that, into the comfort
Of knowing where we were in magnitude's
Designs, plumb in the middest of the points
Halfway between those images of small
And great so intense that they could hardly make
Sense as size at all: measure was what
The humankindness of our height was for.

No. Not the wheels without wheels and within,
But the old rondure of it, the disdain
Of cold circumference for the hopefulness
Of making any point on it an archon,
An upstart tyrant called "Begin" or "12
O'clock" or "0 Degrees" (or "360",
As he is also known in learned circles).
There is but one true point of origin
Each circle knows, and hides from all desire.
There is no kingdom of periphery,
Only the terrible matter of return.

Wherever, whenever, whatever, the darkness we started
Out of, as if at a shout, was only the shadow
Of something looming, something already there.

AFTERNOON AND AFTERWARDS

Spinnakers dot the blue-green Sound
(*As much as to say, the wind has held*)
The cicadas sing upon the ground
(*As much as to say, the trees are felled*)
Dry drops fall as the peas are shelled
(*As much as to say, they'll soon be drowned*)
What the stars marked the sunlight quelled
(*As much as to say, the world is round*).
The clouds hung low, the high wind howled
(*As much as to say, the branch would bend*)
The mast is down, the lines are fouled
(*As much as to say, we have lost a friend*)
There's little to get and less to spend
(*As much as to say, this must be the end*).

COORDINATING CONJUNCTION

And ... and so it goes:
As the thread outlasts the spool,
So the thorn, the rose.

Time observes its rule:
Each instant leaps back into
The dark lilied pool

It sprang from. Each blue
Tile along the garden wall
Ends where it has to

End, in a thin scrawl
Of grout that marks out its grave.
Summer comes to fall.

Though breathing and brave,
The sentence stops, that must burn
The air in its cave.

Thus our great concern—
Feeling shut in by the wall
Of our own pattern—

Seems quite natural:
Even with some makeshift plan,
How to keep it all

Going, how to fan
The embers of aftermath
Up now into an

Even flame—not wrath
Nor sudden lust yielded to—
But light on a path

That would continue
Until some kind of an end
Crept up into view

From around some bend
Or straight toward us from the dark.
Who but would extend

That path, keep the spark
Still left glowing, nursed along
A last walk through stark

Finality? (Strong
Last words will count more than fond
Scraps of sometime song).

Reaching out beyond
A last bit, we understand,
Breaks some kind of bond:

Desperate, a hand
Trembling adds yets one more *and*
And *and*, and *and*, and

THE MAD POTTER

Now at the turn of the year this coil of clay
Bites its own tail: a New Year starts to choke
On the old one's ragged end. I bite my tongue
As the end of me—of my rope of stuff and nonsense
(The nonsense held, it was the stuff that broke),
Of bones and light, of levity and crime,
Of reddish clay and hope—still bides its time.

» «

Each of my pots is quite unusable,
Even for contemplating as an object
Of gross unuse. In its own mode of being
Useless, though, each of them remains unique,
Subject to nothing, and themselves unseeing,
Stronger by virtue of what makes them weak.

» «

I pound at all my clay. I pound the air.
This senseless lump, slapped into something like
Something, sits bound around by my despair.
For even as the great Creator's free
Hand shapes the forms of life, so—what? This pot,
Unhollowed solid, too full of itself,
Runneth over with incapacity.
I put it with the others on the shelf.

» «

These tiny cups will each provide one sip
Of what's inside them, aphoristic prose
Unwilling, like full arguments, to make
Its points, then join them in extended lines
Like long draughts from the bowl of a deep lake.
The honey of knowledge, like my milky slip,
Firms slowly up against what merely flows.

» «

Some of my older pieces bore inscriptions
That told a story only when you'd learned
How not to read them: LIVE reverted to EVIL,
EROS kept running backwards into SORE.
Their words, all fired up for truth, got burned.
I'll not write on weak vessels any more.

» «

My juvenilia? I gave them names
In those days: Hans was all handles and no spout;
Bernie believed the whole world turned about
Himself alone; Sadie was close to James
(But Herman touched her bottom when he could);
Paul fell to pieces; Peter wore away
To nothing; Len was never any good;
Alf was a flat, random pancake, May
An opened blossom; Bud was an ash-tray.
Even their names break off, though: Whatsisface,
That death-mask of Desire, and—you know!—
The smaller version of that (Oh, what was it?—
You know ...) All of my pots now have to go
By number only. Which is no disgrace.

» «

Begin with being—in an anagram
Of unending—conclude in some dark den;
This is no matter. What I've been, I am:
What I will be is what I make of all
This clay, this moment. Now begin again ...
Poured out of emptiness, drop by slow drop,
I start up at the quarreling sounds of water.
Pots cry out silently at me to stop.

» «

What are we like? A barrelfull of this
Oozy wet substance, shadow-crammed, whose smudges
Of darkness lurk within but rise to kiss
The fingers that disturb the gentle edges
Of their bland world of shapelessness and bliss.

» «

The half-formed cup cries out in agony,
The lump of clay suffers a silent pain.
I heard the cup, though, full of feeling, say
"O clay be true, O clay keep constant to
Your need to take, again and once again,
This pounding from your mad creator who
Only stops hurting when he's hurting you."

» «

What will I then have left behind me? Over
The years I have originated some
Glazes that wear away at what they cover
And weep for what they never can become.
My Deadware, widely imitated; blue
Skyware of an amazing lightness; tired
Hopeware that I abandoned for my own
Good reasons; Hereware; Thereware; ware that grew
Weary of everything that earth desired;
Hellware that dances while it's being fired,
Noware that vanishes while being thrown.

» «

Appearing to be silly, wisdom survives
Like tribes of superseded gods who go
Hiding in caves of triviality
From which they laughingly control our lives.
So with my useless pots: safe from the blow
Of carelessness, or outrage at their flaws,
They brave time's lion and his smashing paws.

—All of which tempts intelligence to call
Pure uselessness one more commodity.
The Good-for-Nothing once became our Hero,
But images of him, laid-back, carelessly
Laughing, were upright statues after all.
From straight above, each cup adds up to zero.

»   «

Clay to clay: Soon I shall indeed become
Dumb as these solid cups of hardened mud
(Dull *terra cruda* colored like our blood);
Meanwhile the slap and thump of palm and thumb
On wet mis-shapenness begins to hum
With meaning that was silent for so long.
The words of my wheel's turning come to ring
Truer than Truth itself does, my great *Ding
Dong-an-sich* that echoes everything
(Against it even lovely bells ring wrong):
Its whole voice gathers up the purest parts
Of all our speech, the vowels of the earth,
The aspirations of our hopeful hearts
Or the prophetic sibillance of song.

NOTES

KINNERET   The disjunct form of these quatrains is borrowed from the Malay *pantun* (not from its fussy, refrain-plagued nineteenth-century French derivative, the *pantoum*): the first and second lines frame one sentence, and the next two another, apparently unrelated, one. The two are superficially connected by cross-rhyming, and by some common construction, scheme, pun, assonance, or the like and, below the surface, by some puzzlingly deeper parable. Thus a self-descriptive example:

CATAMARAN

Pantuns in the original Malay
   Are quatrains of two thoughts, but of one mind.
Athwart these two pontoons I sail away,
   Yet touching neither; land lies far behind.

FROM THE INNER CITY   I may have been thinking, in writing the second strophe, of how the Russian armies stood waiting, across the Vistula from Warsaw, for the fleeing Germans to level the city and decimate the remaining pool of Polish officers and administrators.

A GARDEN IN PASADENA   Mt. Wilson is the site of a less and less useful astronomical observatory.

THE TRIMMER   The "hammered, red sickle" and "far-reaching green, crescent scimitar" are the emblematic swords of the Politburo and the Prophet.

MORE QUATRAINS FROM HARP LAKE   See note to "Kinneret."

MARKS AND NOISES   The first four lines recall a discussion by Eric A. Havelock.

TO A SCULPTOR   Pliny's account is in Book XXXV of his *Natural History*, ¶43.

EFFET DE NEIGE   *M. Chose* is French for *Whatsisname*; *M. Machine* would be a shade more formal for the same.

AN OLD ENGRAVING   A *memento mori* by Hans Sebald Beham (1500–1550).

THE WIDENER BURYING-GROUND   "He who packs, with a glowing faith . . ." see the motto below Sargent's mural on the landing of Widener Library at Harvard: "Happy he who with a glowing faith / In one embrace clasps Death and Victory"

TO ELIZABETH BISHOP   The first four tercets were sent to the addressee on a postcard, in re her splendid "The Moose". The additional lines, written some years later, explain themselves. The poem of Frost referred to in them, itself an answer to Wordsworth's "The Boy of Winander", is "The Most of It."

John Hollander's first book of poems, A CRACKLING OF THORNS, *was chosen by W. H. Auden as the 1958 volume in the Yale Series of Younger Poets;* MOVIE-GOING AND OTHER POEMS *appeared in 1962,* VISIONS FROM THE RAMBLE *in 1965,* TYPES OF SHAPE *in 1969,* THE NIGHT MIRROR *in 1971,* TALES TOLD OF THE FATHERS *in 1975,* REFLECTIONS ON ESPIONAGE *in 1976,* SPECTRAL EMANATIONS *in 1978,* BLUE WINE *in 1979,* POWERS OF THIRTEEN *in 1983 and* IN TIME AND PLACE *in 1986. He has written four books of criticism,* THE UNTUNING OF THE SKY, VISION AND RESONANCE, RHYME'S REASON *and* THE FIGURE OF ECHO *and edited both* THE LAUREL BEN JONSON *and, with Harold Bloom,* THE WIND AND THE RAIN, *an anthology of verse for young people, an anthology of contemporary poetry,* POEMS OF OUR MOMENT *and was a co-editor of* THE OXFORD ANTHOLOGY OF ENGLISH LITERATURE. *He is the editor (with Anthony Hecht, with whom he shared the Bollingen Prize in Poetry in 1983) of* JIGGERY-POKERY: A COMPENDIUM OF DOUBLE DACTYLS. *Mr. Hollander attended Columbia and Indiana Universities, was a junior fellow of the Society of Fellows of Harvard University, and taught at Connecticut College and Yale, and was Professor of English at Hunter College and the Graduate Center,* CUNY. *He is currently A. Bartlett Giamatti Professor of English at Yale.*

A NOTE ON THE TYPE

This book was set on the Linotype in Granjon, a type named in compliment to Robert Granjon but neither a copy of a classic face nor an entirely original creation. George W. Jones based his designs on the type used by Claude Garamond (c. 1480–1561) in his beautiful French books. Granjon more closely resembles Garamond's own type than does any of the various modern types that bear his name.

Robert Granjon began his career as type cutter in 1523. The boldest and most original designer of his time, he was one of the first to practice the trade of type founder apart from that of printer. Between 1557 and 1562 Granjon printed about twenty books in types designed by himself, following, after the fashion, the cursive handwriting of the time. These types, usually known as *caractères de civilité*, he himself called *lettres françaises*, as especially appropriate to his own country.

Composition by Heritage Printers, Inc.,
Charlotte, North Carolina
Printing and binding by Halliday Lithographers,
West Hanover, Massachusetts
Designed by Harry Ford